AF270401

WONDERFUL WORKING DOGS

Written by Annabel Griffin

Illustrated by Marina Halak

CONTENTS

Words in **BOLD** can be found in the glossary.

THE WORLD OF DOGS

Get ready to explore the wonderful world of working dogs! From the herding sheepdogs to the guarding great danes, there are so many different types of lovable working dogs to discover.

WHERE DO DOGS COME FROM?

Believe it or not, all dogs are **descendants** of ancient wolves. The details of how and when wolves became dogs are still quite foggy, but it likely started when humans began to **domesticate** and train wolves, at least 14,000 years ago. Today, dogs can be found all over the world.

WHAT IS A BREED?

A breed is a particular group of dogs that all share the same (or very similar) appearance and **characteristics**, making them easy to identify. There are hundreds of different breeds, and they can vary wildly in size, shape, hairiness, and personality.

Not all dogs belong to a specific breed. Some dogs, known as mutts or mongrels, are a mixture of lots of different breeds. They can make fantastic pets, and can often be found looking for a loving home at rescue or **rehoming shelters.**

GETTING A DOG?

Maybe you already have a dog in your family, or maybe you'd like to in the future. Owning a dog can be fun and rewarding, but it's also a big responsibility. Some dogs need a lot of space, time and attention. Before buying or **adopting** a dog, you should always carefully research their breed and think about whether you are able to give them everything they need to be happy.

BREED GROUPS

Dog breeds are often arranged into seven different groups that are loosely based on the jobs that they were originally bred to do.

SPORTING GROUP

Also known as gundogs, these dogs were originally bred to help hunters retrieve birds.

NON-SPORTING GROUP

This is the group for dogs that don't fit into any of the other groups, so they are quite a mixed bunch!

TERRIER GROUP

This group were originally bred to hunt burrowing animals, such as rats, rabbits, foxes, and badgers. Most of them have "terrier" as part of their name.

WORKING GROUP

Dogs in this group were originally bred to perform practical tasks, such as pulling sleds and carts. They were also often used as watchdogs. They are usually large dogs.

HOUND GROUP

Hounds were bred for their sense of smell or sight, and were usually used for hunting. They can be split into two sub-groups: sighthounds and scent hounds.

HERDING GROUP

This group includes dogs that were bred to work on farms; herding and guarding livestock, such as sheep and cows.

TOY GROUP

Tiny breeds that are small enough to sit in your lap fall into this group. They are bred mostly as pets and companions.

WONDERFUL WORKING DOGS

Dogs and humans have been working side by side for thousands of years. Many breeds of dog have been designed to be good at specific jobs, such as herding, hunting, and guarding.

Most working dog breeds have a high level of intelligence, energy, and trainability. They can be loyal and loving companions, but often require more time and attention than dogs bred purely for companionship.

Border Collie

Bursting with energy and intelligence, border collies are famous for being excellent sheepdogs. They are very loyal and easy to train, but can become bored easily and need a lot of daily exercise.

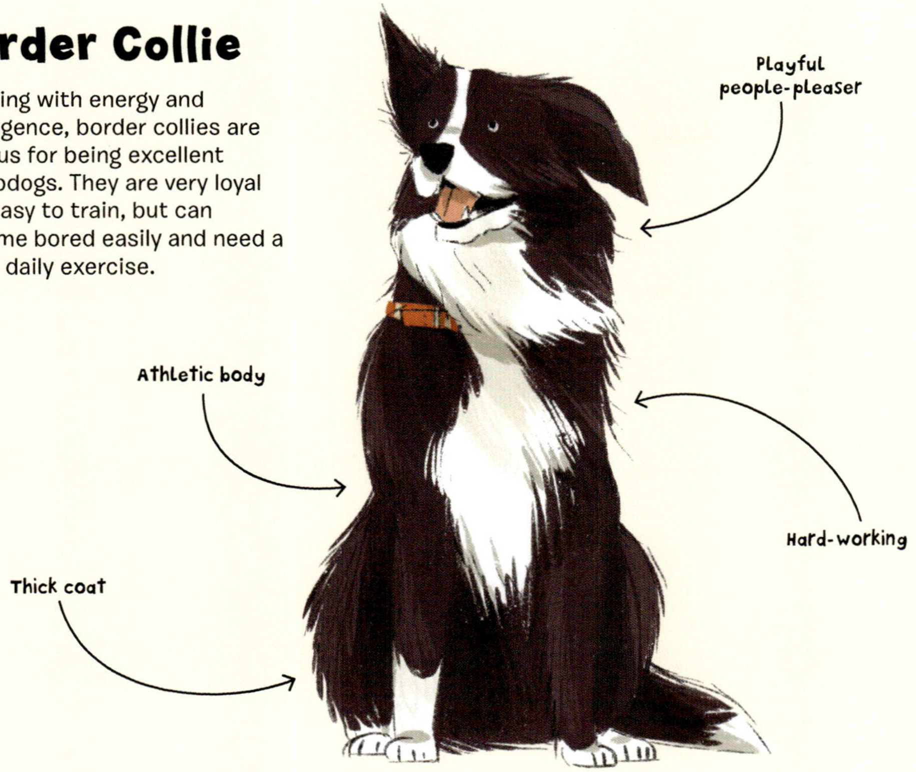

ORIGIN: United Kingdom	
COAT: Medium-length, smooth	
PERSONALITY: Smart and hard-working	

INTELLIGENCE	
ENERGY LEVEL	
TRAINABILITY	

Old English Sheepdog

These giant balls of fluff make great sheepdogs and have even been known to try and herd children! They are friendly, love to explore, and make great walking companions. Their thick coats need a lot of grooming. Some owners actually shave their dog's fur and spin it into yarn!

ORIGIN: United Kingdom

COAT: Long, very thick

PERSONALITY: Gentle and outgoing

INTELLIGENCE

ENERGY LEVEL

TRAINABILITY

Rough Collie

These beautiful dogs were originally bred to herd sheep in Scotland. They are playful, energetic, and easy to train. Like the Old English sheepdog, their long, elegant coat needs a lot of grooming.

ORIGIN: United Kingdom

COAT: Long, very thick

PERSONALITY: Smart and affectionate

INTELLIGENCE

ENERGY LEVEL

TRAINABILITY

Berger Picard
(Picardy Sheepdog)

These scruffy French sheepdogs are now a rare breed. They are funny and loyal, and love to play games. They can make excellent companions for active owners.

ORIGIN: France

COAT: Medium-length, **wiry**

PERSONALITY: Playful but sensitive

INTELLIGENCE	🐾🐾🐾🐾🐾
ENERGY LEVEL	🐾🐾🐾🐾🐾
TRAINABILITY	🐾🐾🐾🐾🐾

Australian Shepherd

Despite the name, the Australian shepherd (or "Aussie") was actually first bred in the USA, in the 1800s, to work on the **ranches**. However, they may have been bred from herding dogs brought over to the USA from Australia and New Zealand. They are still often used as a working dog and are popular with cowhands.

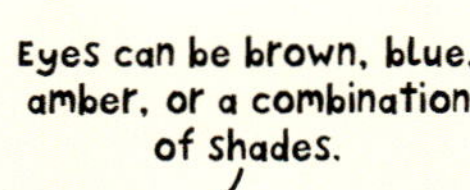

ORIGIN: USA

COAT: Medium-length, thick

PERSONALITY: Active and protective

INTELLIGENCE	
ENERGY LEVEL	
TRAINABILITY	  

Standard Schnauzer

Schnauzers were originally bred as multipurpose farm dogs, with good skills in guarding livestock and rat-catching. They are very intelligent, alert, and protective, making them good watchdogs.

ORIGIN: Germany

COAT: Medium-length, wiry

PERSONALITY: Lively and alert

INTELLIGENCE 🐾🐾🐾🐾🐾

ENERGY LEVEL 🐾🐾🐾🐾🐾

TRAINABILITY 🐾🐾🐾🐾🐾

Puli

Is it a dog or is it a mop? This unusual-looking breed was originally used as a herding dog by the **nomadic** Magyar tribes, who settled in what is now Hungary in the 9th century CE. They make great family pets, but their amazing long coats need a lot of looking after.

ORIGIN: Hungary

COAT: Long, **corded**

PERSONALITY: Fun-loving and friendly

INTELLIGENCE 

ENERGY LEVEL

TRAINABILITY 

Pembrokeshire Welsh Corgi

These dogs are famous for being the beloved pets of Queen Elizabeth II of the United Kingdom, but they were originally bred as cattle-herders and guard dogs in Wales. Despite their short legs, they are surprisingly speedy and athletic.

ORIGIN: United Kingdom

COAT: Medium-length, thick

PERSONALITY: Loving but independent

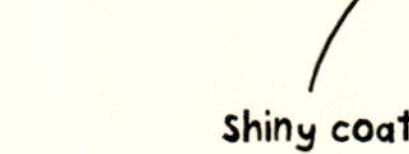

INTELLIGENCE

ENERGY LEVEL

TRAINABILITY

Belgian Shepherd

This hard-working breed are more than just great herding dogs. Belgian shepherds are used for a variety of other jobs, including as **service dogs**, guard dogs, police and military dogs.

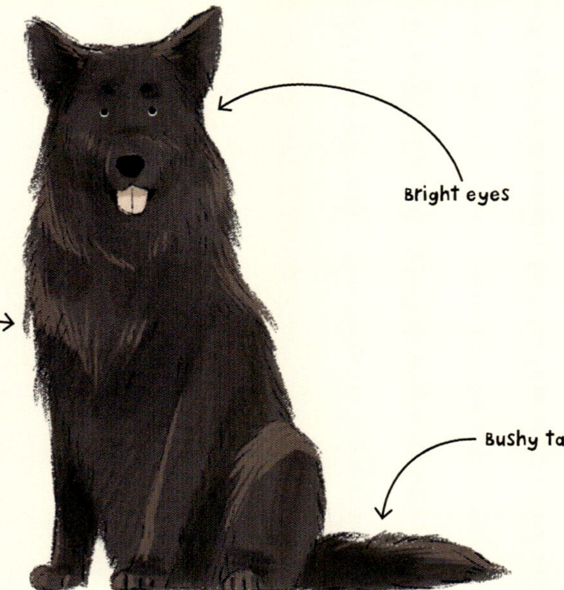

ORIGIN: Belgium

COAT: Long, thick

PERSONALITY: Brave and loyal

INTELLIGENCE

ENERGY LEVEL

TRAINABILITY

German Shepherd

One of the most popular working breeds, the German shepherd is a brilliant all-rounder. As the name suggests, they were originally German herding dogs but can tackle just about any job a dog can do. They are often used for police work, search-and-rescue, and are even taken into war zones by the military. They also make good companion and service dogs, and are popular pets.

ORIGIN: Germany

COAT: Medium-length, thick

PERSONALITY: Confident and brave

INTELLIGENCE

ENERGY LEVEL

TRAINABILITY

Siberian Husky

This well-known dog was first bred by the Chukchi people of Siberia to pull their sleds and for companionship. They are strong dogs, with incredible **endurance** for running long distances in difficult conditions. They are popular pets, but their high-energy, mischievous nature can make them quite a handful.

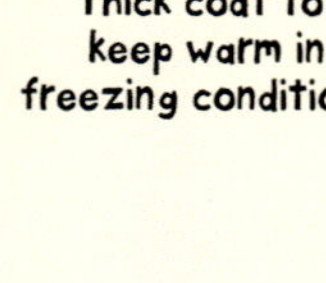

ORIGIN: Siberia

COAT: Medium-length, very thick

PERSONALITY: Friendly and mischievous

INTELLIGENCE

ENERGY LEVEL

TRAINABILITY

Samoyed

This stylish fluffy dog is descended from reindeer herders in Siberia. They were originally used for sled pulling, herding, protection, and hunting.

ORIGIN: Siberia

COAT: Long, very thick

PERSONALITY: Gentle and social

INTELLIGENCE	
ENERGY LEVEL	
TRAINABILITY	

Chinook

The Chinook is a rare breed of American sled dog. They were first bred in New Hampshire by the author and explorer Arthur Treadwell Walden, in the early 20th century. The breed was created by **crossbreeding** a Greenland dog (page 18) with a Mastiff/Saint Bernard cross (pages 21 and 23).

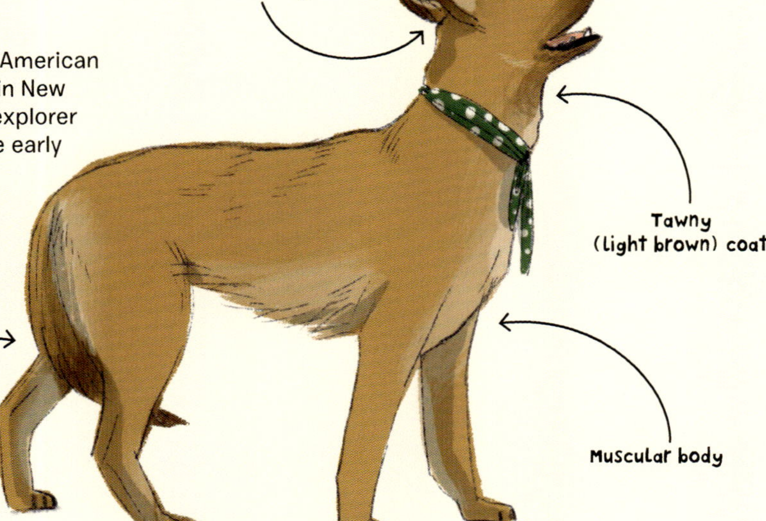

ORIGIN: USA

COAT: Medium-length, thick

PERSONALITY: Patient and loyal

INTELLIGENCE	  
ENERGY LEVEL	
TRAINABILITY	 

Alaskan Malamute

Although they bear many similarities, the Alaskan malamute is bigger, stronger, and fluffier than their close relative, the Siberian husky (page 16). They are also slower. They were bred to carry heavy loads over long distances.

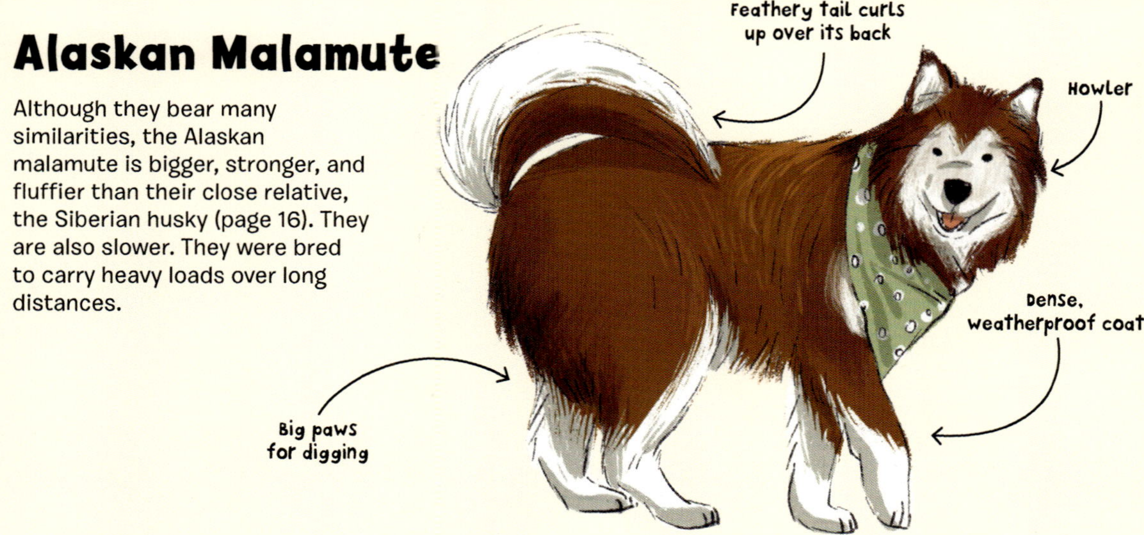

ORIGIN: Alaska

COAT: Medium-length, very thick

PERSONALITY: Playful and loving

INTELLIGENCE	🐾 🐾 🐾 🐾 🐾
ENERGY LEVEL	🐾 🐾 🐾 🐾 🐾
TRAINABILITY	🐾 🐾 🐾 🐾 🐾

Greenland Dog

The Greenland Dog is an ancient sled dog breed, which is thought to have changed very little since it was brought to Greenland from Siberia by the Thule people 1,000 years ago. **Genetically,** it is now considered the same breed as the Canadian Eskimo dog.

ORIGIN: Greenland

COAT: Medium-length, very thick

PERSONALITY: Loyal and good-natured

INTELLIGENCE	🐾 🐾 🐾 🐾 🐾
ENERGY LEVEL	🐾 🐾 🐾 🐾 🐾
TRAINABILITY	🐾 🐾 🐾 🐾 🐾

Bernese Mountain Dog

These dogs were bred to pull carts in the Swiss Alps. They were also used as farm dogs. They are gentle giants who love being outdoors.

ORIGIN: Switzerland

COAT: Long, thick

PERSONALITY: Calm and strong

INTELLIGENCE

ENERGY LEVEL

TRAINABILITY

Bouvier des Flandres

This big shaggy dog started out as a farm dog in Flanders, Belgium. It was used for herding and pulling carts. They also make excellent guard and watchdogs.

ORIGIN: Belgium

COAT: Medium-length, thick, wavy

PERSONALITY: Fearless and independent

INTELLIGENCE 

ENERGY LEVEL 

TRAINABILITY 

Rottweiler

The size, obedience, and fearlessness of Rottweilers makes them excellent guard and security dogs. They may look big and scary, but they can be gentle and loving family pets. They can also have a very playful, silly side.

ORIGIN: Germany

COAT: Short, smooth

PERSONALITY: Gentle and obedient

INTELLIGENCE

ENERGY LEVEL

TRAINABILITY

Boxer

Boxers were originally bred as hunting dogs in the 19th century. They are strong, alert, and suspicious of strangers, making them great guard dogs. They are very affectionate with their owners.

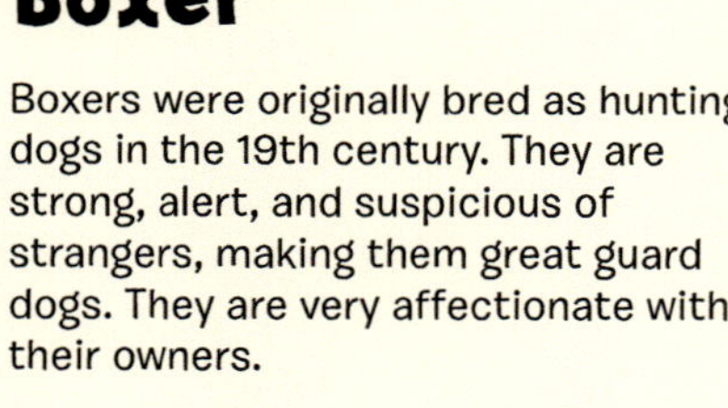

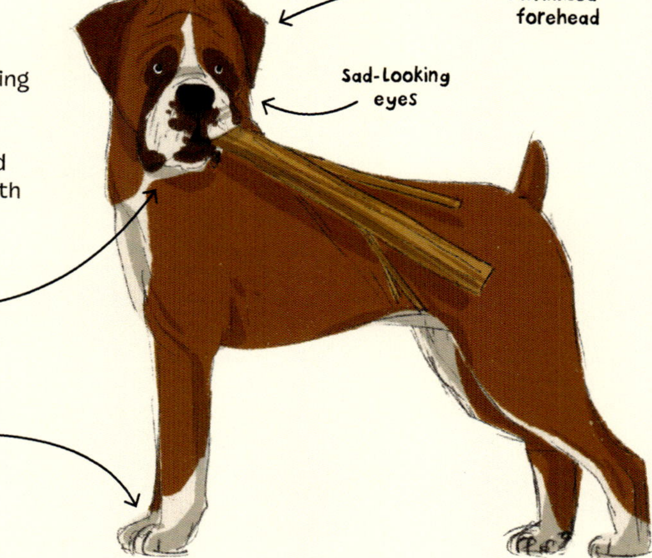

ORIGIN: Germany

COAT: Short, smooth

PERSONALITY: Fun-loving and alert

INTELLIGENCE

ENERGY LEVEL

TRAINABILITY

Great Dane

Great Danes are one of the largest breeds of dog and can measure up to 35 inches (90cm) in height. It's no wonder they make good guard dogs, since their size could scare off any intruder! Don't be fooled; they're really gentle giants.

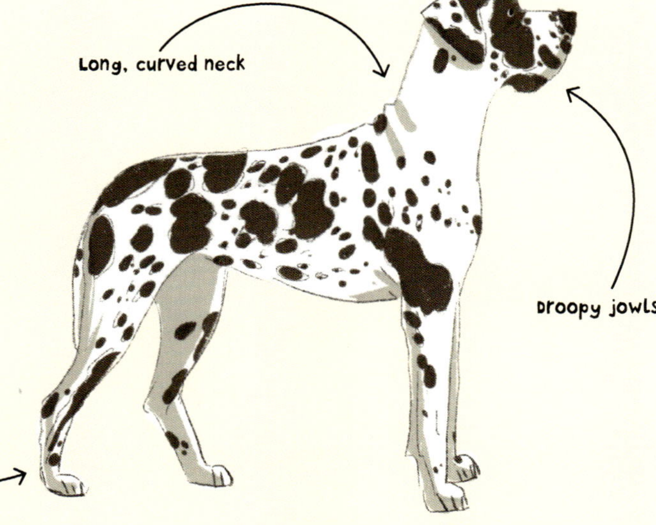

ORIGIN: Germany

COAT: Short, smooth

PERSONALITY: Friendly and reliable

INTELLIGENCE

ENERGY LEVEL

TRAINABILITY

Mastiff

These mighty dogs have descended from ancient hunting dogs introduced to Britain by the Romans. They have a history of being loyal guardians and protectors. They are very large and weigh 120–230 pounds (54–104kg).

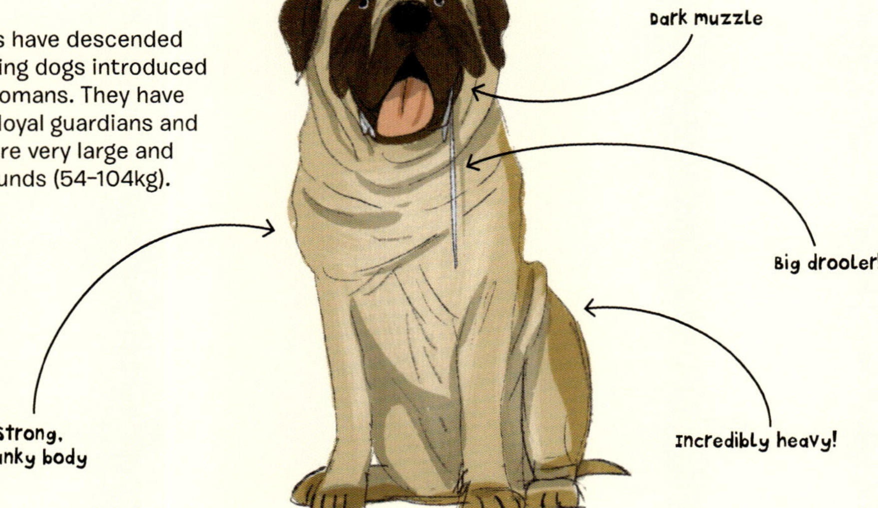

ORIGIN: United Kingdom

COAT: Short, smooth

PERSONALITY: Protective and loyal

INTELLIGENCE

ENERGY LEVEL

TRAINABILITY

Dobermann (Doberman Pinscher)

This breed have brilliant guarding and tracking skills. They are also speedy and very intelligent. It's no wonder they make good police dogs! They love being part of an active family.

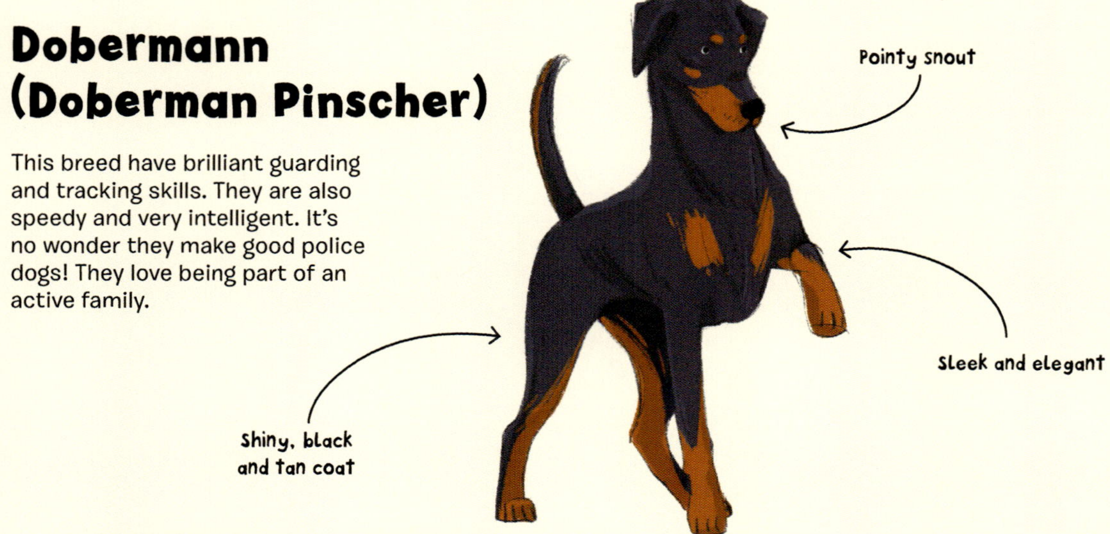

ORIGIN: Germany

COAT: Short, smooth

PERSONALITY: Alert and fearless

INTELLIGENCE 🐾🐾🐾🐾🐾

ENERGY LEVEL 🐾🐾🐾🐾🐾

TRAINABILITY 🐾🐾🐾🐾🐾

Airedale Terrier

Sometimes called "The King of the Terriers", airedales are the largest of the terrier breeds (see page 6). They were originally bred for hunting, but have a strong history as police and military dogs. In World War I, they were used to carry messages to soldiers behind enemy lines.

ORIGIN: United Kingdom

COAT: Short/medium-length, wiry

PERSONALITY: Sporty and determined

INTELLIGENCE 🐾🐾🐾🐾🐾

ENERGY LEVEL 🐾🐾🐾🐾🐾

TRAINABILITY 🐾🐾🐾🐾🐾

Saint Bernard

This massive dog was originally bred by the monks of the Great Saint Bernard Hospice in the Swiss Alps as guard dogs, but were later used for mountain rescue. They would face difficult and dangerous conditions to rescue people lost in the mountains.

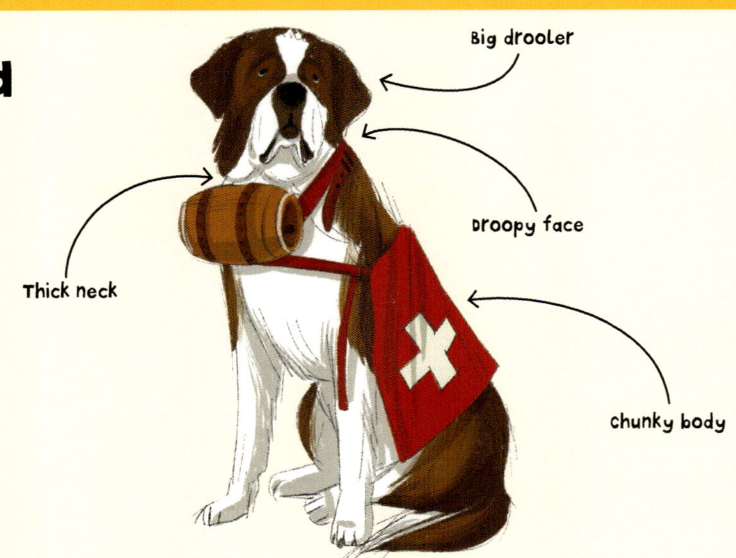

ORIGIN: Switzerland

COAT: Short, thick

PERSONALITY: Caring and gentle

INTELLIGENCE	
ENERGY LEVEL	
TRAINABILITY	

Newfoundland

These big softies were originally bred as fishermen's dogs, to help retrieve nets. Their strength, courage, and swimming skills make them excellent lifesaving, water rescue dogs.

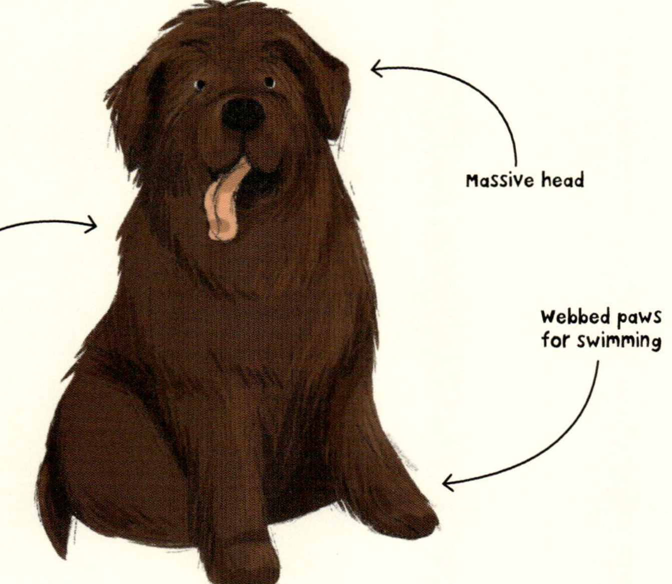

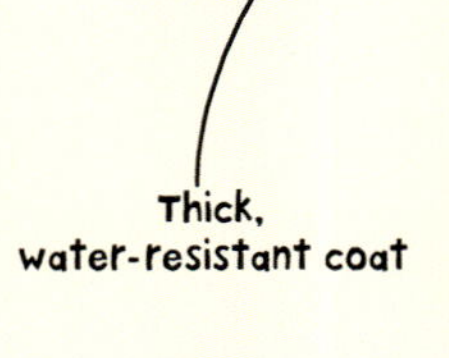

ORIGIN: Canada

COAT: Long, very thick

PERSONALITY: Sweet and calm

INTELLIGENCE	
ENERGY LEVEL	
TRAINABILITY	

WHAT'S THAT DOG?

Now that you have read all about hard-working dogs, how good are you at identifying them? There are 25 different dogs to figure out. Use the information in the book to help you.

1

What am I?
A. Siberian Husky
B. Greenland Dog
C. Chinook

2

What am I?
A. Saint Bernard
B. Newfoundland
C. Mastiff

3

What am I?
A. Puli
B. Standard Schnauzer
C. Airedale Terrier

4

What am I?
A. Boxer
B. Old English Sheepdog
C. Saint Bernard

5

What am I?
A. Siberian Husky
B. Puli
C. Samoyed

6

What am I?
A. Australian Shepherd
B. Rough Collie
C. Berger Picard

7

What am I?
A. Corgi
B. Standard Schnauzer
C. Puli

8

What am I?
A. Australian Shepherd
B. Old English Sheepdog
C. German Shepherd

9

What am I?
A. Australian Shepherd
B. Border Collie
C. Belgian Shepherd

10

What am I?
A. Samoyed
B. Alaskan Malamute
C. Bernese
   Mountain Dog

11

What am I?
A. Rough Collie
B. Border Collie
C. Berger Picard

12

What am I?
A. Australian Shepherd
B. Old English Sheepdog
C. Standard Schnauzer

13

What am I?
A. Alaskan Malamute
B. Corgi
C. Great Dane

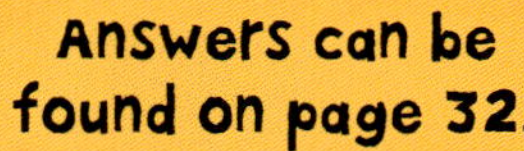

14

What am I?
A. Siberian Husky
B. German Shepherd
C. Chinook

15

What am I?
A. Bouvier Des Flandres
B. Greenland Dog
C. Belgian Shepherd

16

What am I?
A. Corgi
B. Puli
C. Standard Schnauzer

17

What am I?
A. Dobermann
B. Old English Sheepdog
C. Border Collie

18

What am I?
A. Airedale Terrier
B. Dobermann
C. Rottweiler

19

What am I?
A. Boxer
B. Rough Collie
C. Berger Picard

20

What am I?
A. Rottweiler
B. Great Dane
C. Boxer

21

What am I?
A. Chinook
B. Mastiff
C. Alaskan Malamute

22

What am I?
A. German Shepherd
B. Mastiff
C. Samoyed

23

What am I?
A. Dobermann
B. Greenland Dog
C. Husky

24

What am I?
A. Bernese
   Mountain Dog
B. Newfoundland
C. Mastiff

25

What am I?
A. Chinook
B. Great Dane
C. Bouvier Des Flandres

SPOT THE DOG

There are so many brilliant dogs in the world. You can see them everywhere you go: in towns, parks, and sometimes even at the beach! See which of these are the most popular dogs where you live, make a note of them in a journal if you do spot them.

Which dogs do you think will be the most and least common in your area? Write your guesses in a journal and check if you were right. You may be suprised how many you spot, now that you know your breeds!

Border Collie

Pembrokeshire Welsh Corgi

Standard Schnauzer

Saint Bernard

Puli

Samoyed

Australian Shepherd

Old English Sheepdog

Rough Collie

Mastiff

Dobermann

Newfoundland

HEROIC DOGS

Man's best friend and man's hero. Take a look at these amazing stories from some of the world's smartest and bravest dogs.

Mountain Rescuer

Barry, a Saint Bernard from Switzerland, saved the lives of more than 40 people. He lived in the Swiss Alps in the 1800s, and rescued people lost in mountain snow storms. He is still one of the bravest dogs ever! There's even a Saint Bernard Rescue Foundation named after him!

Military Hero

One of the most successful military dogs ever, Lucca, was trained to sniff out explosives. Lucca worked on 400 missions, found 40 explosives, and saved hundreds of lives. She was the first U.S. dog to receive the Dickin Medal for bravery.

Firefighter

Eve, a rottweiler from the US, saved her owner Kathie, who was **paralyzed** from the waist down, from a burning van. Eve dragged Kathie to safety, saving them both from the fire!

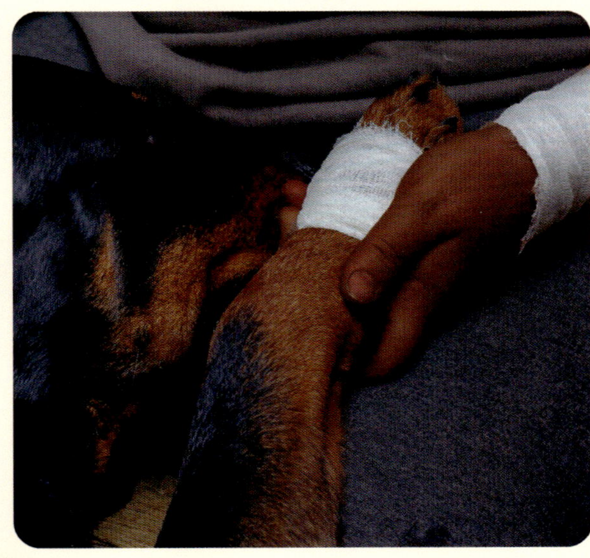

Seaside Lifesavers

Whizz, a Newfoundland from the UK, worked for 10 years as a water rescue dog. In total, he saved 9 people and a dog from drowning! He was given an award for his bravery and lifesaving work.

GLOSSARY

Adopting – Legally taking on the animal as your own, receiving all responsibility.

Agility (dog sport) – a sport where dogs complete complicated obstacle courses, including objects that they have run through, around, under, or jump over.

Characteristics – a feature or quality of a person, place, or thing.

Corded – a type of dog coat that forms into long rope-like strands, similar to dreadlocks.

Crossbreeding (crossbreeds) – when two dogs of different breeds have puppies.

Descendants – people or animals that are related to an individual or group who lived in the past. For example, you are a descendant of your parents and grandparents.

Domesticate – to be tamed or trained to live or work with humans.

Endurance – the ability or strength to continue doing something for a long time.

Genetically – how our genes carry information from parents to children.

Instinct – when an animal does something without being trained. They naturally know what to do or how to react to a situation.

Nomadic – nomadic people move around from place to place, with no fixed home.

Paralyzed – when someone is unable to move a specific part of their body, usually as a result of illness or injury.

Ranches – large farms for raising horses, cattle or sheep (usually in Mexico, Western United States or Western Canada).

Rehoming shelter – a place where dogs (or other animals) who were lost, stray, or given up by their owners, are looked after until they can be adopted into a new home.

Service dog (or assistance dog) – a dog that has been trained to assist a person with a disability. Examples of service dogs include guide dogs, hearing dogs, medical response dogs, and autism service dogs.

Underbite (or undershot) – when the lower jaw or teeth stick out in front of the upper jaw or teeth, when the mouth is closed.

Wiry – a type of dog coat that is rough, thick, and bristly.

INDEX

WHAT'S THAT DOG ANSWERS

1 - B. Greenland dog
2 - B. Newfoundland
3 - C. Airedale Terrier
4 - C. Saint Bernard
5 - A. Siberian Husky
6 - C. Berger Picard
7 - C. Puli
8 - B. Old English Sheepdog
9 - A. Australian Shepherd
10 - A. Samoyed
11 - A. Rough Collie
12 - C. Standard Schnauzer
13 - A. Alaskan Malamute
14 - B. German Shepherd
15 - C. Belgian Shepherd
16 - A. Corgi
17 - C. Border Collie
18 - C. Rottweiler
19 - A. Boxer
20 - B. Great Dane
21 - A. Chinook
22 - B. Mastiff
23 - A. Dobermann
24 - A. Bernese Mountain dog
25 - C. Bouvier Des Flandres

ABOUT THE AUTHOR

Annabel is a writer and artist based in London, UK. Having worked as a bookseller for many years, she now writes children's books focusing on animals and the natural world. Her recent titles include *What Can I See in the Wild?*, *Seasons* and *The Spectacular Lives of Sharks*.

ABOUT THE ILLUSTRATOR

Marina is a talented illustrator of children's books from Ukraine. Her stunning illustrations are inspired by her own childhood, children, nature, magical moments and fairytales.